Manifestations and Prophetic Symbolism in a Move of the Spirit

MANIFESTATIONS AND PROPHETIC SYMBOLISM IN A MOVE OF THE SPIRIT

John Arnott

New Wine Press

New Wine Ministries
PO Box 17
Chichester
West Sussex
United Kingdom
PO19 2AW

ISBN 978-1-905991-27-3

Typeset by CRB Associates, Reepham, Norfolk
Cover design by CCD, www.ccdgroup.co.uk
Printed in the United States of America

CONTENTS

WHY MANIFESTATIONS?

Over the years, one of the most frequently raised issues concerning the revival that began in Toronto in 1994 has been that of the manifestations that occur when people are touched by the power of God. For that reason I have, for a long time, wanted to find the time to write a short book that deals with this issue from a number of perspectives. The first and most obvious question is: why do manifestations occur? Secondly, is there anything we can learn from them about what is happening to the person experiencing them? And thirdly, when revival breaks out and the Holy Spirit seems to be the only One in control, how does a pastor handle that? These are the questions that I will attempt to answer in the first section of this book. In the second section we will look at the separate but closely linked topic of "prophetic symbolism".

GOD LIKES FEELINGS!

Though it might seem obvious to some, it is worth reminding ourselves that God is an emotional God. Throughout the Bible you can see that He expresses a full range of emotions: love, compassion, anger, sorrow, even regret (1 Samuel 15:11). Some Christians don't necessarily think of God as being emotional, so they struggle with the idea that God has made *us* emotional beings and expects us to express the full range of human emotions. But God created emotions to give life a color and richness that would be otherwise lacking. Being emotional is not something God frowns upon – He actually wants us to embrace our humanity, not suppress it. For love and intimacy to take effect, our emotions are indispensable.

I'm always fascinated whenever I see the latest robotic technology that scientists have dreamed up. Robots are so advanced these days that they can emulate human movement fairly convincingly. But one thing scientists and engineers have never mastered is getting a robot to reproduce accurate facial expressions. You can't look at a robot and tell whether he is angry, happy, tired or wide awake. A robot simply cannot express emotions and feelings like a human. So let's remember, we are not robots! God made us in such a way that what we are experiencing on the inside shows up on the outside. Emotions are the visible signals that indicate what is taking place in our hearts.

Given this, we should not be surprised when people who are being touched by the power of God have a strong emotional response to the experience. When God touches us by the power of His Holy Spirit it has a deep emotional impact and our reaction to that will vary. Often, how we react will depend on what particular issue God is dealing with at that time. It may be appropriate to laugh, cry or shout – and these would be "appropriate" responses because God is not shocked or offended by our emotions.

SHOULD WE "FEEL" THE HOLY SPIRIT?

The Bible talks about an experience called the "baptism of the Holy Spirit". The word translated "baptism" means to be "completely immersed" in the power and presence of the Living God. In Toronto, over the years, we have witnessed many people being gloriously immersed in God's presence and our observations have caused us to use words like "soaked", "marinated", and even "pickled", to try to describe what we have seen happening. What quickly became obvious to me was that no one could experience God's presence to that degree and *not* react either physically or emotionally. John the Baptist, speaking about Jesus, described Him as the One who would, *"baptize you with the Holy Spirit and with fire"* (Luke 3:16). I don't know about you, but to me that sounds like something we should be able to feel!

There has, however, in Christian tradition, been a strong resistance to the idea of "emotionalism". Why are Christians so hung up on emotions? I believe it is because we have been conditioned, especially in the West, to be skeptical about everything, to rationalize every experience, and to not trust our emotions. Many Western Christians have very little expectation of God touching them supernaturally, so they begin from a position of doubt and say things like: "You don't necessarily feel anything when God touches you . . . it's not about feelings and emotions . . . you have to receive from God by faith . . . " Of course, I accept that all these statements are true to a point, but it is a mistake to ignore or suppress the emotional aspect of our nature that God created us with. We were designed to "feel" the presence of the Living God, because God is a person! Emotionalism in that sense is not wrong. I am not, by this, endorsing excessive "fleshly" over-emotional behavior that originates in our own soul.

God is love and His greatest desire is for us to love Him with all our heart and soul. That is the very foundation of our relationship with Him. What kind of a relationship would it be if we didn't ever *feel* anything? Love has to be felt, be experienced and reciprocated. When God comes upon a person and overwhelms them with His presence, if that person doesn't feel anything, that would be the exception rather than the norm. Having said that, there are some people who don't react emotionally to God's touch, don't fall over under the power of the Spirit or feel anything in particular – and oddly enough I'm one of them! In order to really feel God's presence I have to go "off duty" and focus intently on the Lord for a time. My wife, Carol, on the other hand, is very spiritually sensitive and reacts a great deal to God's touch.

One of the reasons that I don't react in the same way as Carol when God's presence is evident is that I have a natural tendency towards analyzing things. During the early days of the revival I spent a lot of time looking at people, wondering what was happening in their hearts and generally being curious. It never occurred to me initially that God wanted to have some time alone with *me* – just me and Him, no distractions. Analytical people who spend a lot of time watching those around them tend to ignore their own feelings and this is one reason why this type of person might find it hard to receive from God for themselves. It requires a degree of self-discipline to say, "I'm going to ignore what's going on around me and focus on God. I can analyze it later, but for now I'm going to receive what God has for me." That's what I have had to do and maybe you need to do that too.

SOME BIBLICAL EXAMPLES

It has been helpful for me personally to realize that God is an emotional God, and I hope it is liberating for many to read that God is not offended by our emotions, but I am not trying to build my argument solely on that point. The fact is, there are many examples in Scripture of people being touched by the power of God and deeply affected, either physically or emotionally, as a result.

In the opening chapter of his Gospel, Luke recounts the story of Zechariah the priest. Zechariah and his wife Elizabeth couldn't have children. They were both advanced in years and must have given up on the idea long ago. Then one day, when Zechariah was on duty at the temple, an angel of the Lord appeared right alongside him at the altar of incense. Noticing his shock the angel spoke to him and said,

> *"Do not be afraid, Zechariah; your prayer has been heard. Your wife Elizabeth will bear you a son, and you are to give him the name John."*
>
> (LUKE 1:13)

Zechariah is so surprised that he just can't believe what he is hearing. "How can this be?" he thinks.

> *"Zechariah asked the angel, 'How can I be sure of this? I am an old man and my wife is well along in years.'"*
>
> (LUKE 1:18)

This was the angel's response and the outcome of this divine encounter:

> *"The angel answered, 'I am Gabriel. I stand in the presence of God, and I have been sent to speak to you and to tell you this good news. And now you will be silent and not able to speak until*

*the day this happens, because you did not believe my words, which
will come true at their proper time.'*

*Meanwhile, the people were waiting for Zechariah and
wondering why he stayed so long in the temple. When he came
out, he could not speak to them. They realized he had seen a
vision in the temple, for he kept making signs to them but
remained unable to speak."*

(LUKE 1:19–22)

Let's put ourselves in Zechariah's position now. He
emerges from the temple with a look of shock on his face.
Someone asks him, "Why were you in the temple so long?"
Zechariah can't speak, so he makes a noise, "Mmmmm!"
and begins gesturing with his hands. Maybe he writes
something down for his colleagues at the temple to read
and they begin to understand he's seen a heavenly vision.
Then he goes home and he still can't speak. A week goes
by, nothing, no words come out of his mouth. He com-
municates with his wife, Elizabeth, by sign language and
writing things down. The next thing this couple realize is
that Elizabeth is pregnant!

What would you think if someone you knew came home
from a religious meeting and they couldn't speak? They
could eat, sleep, do everything else they needed to do, but
they couldn't speak. Would you think that's a bad thing or a
good thing? Some of their friends might say, "That's
terrible, it must be demonic. Why would God want to stop
them from speaking?" and here we touch upon another
interesting issue. Many Christians are fond of saying,
"The Holy Spirit is a gentleman. He will never do anything
to you against your will." I agree that the Holy Spirit is
usually gentle – it is one of the fruits of the Spirit – but
it is equally clear in Scripture that He is the Sovereign God
and can do whatever He wants! Did Zechariah want to be
struck dumb for the duration of Elizabeth's pregnancy?

No, of course not, but it was a result of his encounter with God.

This was a highly unusual manifestation resulting from God's touch, but there are numerous other examples in Scripture that are more common, such as falling over under the power of God [1] Here are a few examples:

Genesis 15:12 says, *"As the sun was setting, Abram fell into a deep sleep, and a thick and dreadful darkness came over him."* This was no ordinary sleep. The context of this event shows that God caused Abram to fall into this deep sleep so that He could speak to him in a vision. God was interacting with Abram and an awesome covenant was about to be formed.

Let's transfer that thought into our context. A person is overwhelmed by the presence of God in a meeting and they lie down on the floor. They appear to be fast asleep but they are most likely interacting with God in some way. We should not be surprised when that person gets up and testifies to having had a deep touch from God or that God has healed them of some longstanding emotional hurt. We can see that such a thing is possible right here in Genesis.

We read that Daniel had a similar experience. Daniel heard the voice of God instructing the angel Gabriel to explain the meaning of a vision that Daniel had received. Daniel says,

> *"As he [Gabriel] came near the place where I was standing, I was terrified and fell prostrate ... while he was speaking to me, I was in a deep sleep, with my face to the ground. Then he touched me and raised me to my feet."*
>
> (DANIEL 8:17–18)

---

1. For a fuller examination of manifestations in the Bible, Francis McNutt's book, *Overcome by the Spirit* (Chosen Books, Grand Rapids) is very helpful.

The Scriptures go on to say that after this encounter, *"I, Daniel, was exhausted and lay ill for several days"* (Daniel 8:27).

1 Kings 8:11 and 2 Chronicles 5:14, speaking about the priests at the inauguration of Solomon's temple, both say,

> *"The priests could not perform their service because of the cloud, for the glory of the LORD filled the temple of God."*

Picture the scene: the fact that King Solomon has built a new temple for the glory of the Lord is a really big deal. It has taken seven years to complete and it is magnificent, without equal, filled with cedar and gold. An elaborate ceremony is planned for its opening; all the priests of God have new robes; the whole nation of Israel is gathered to witness this momentous occasion and it is heralded with trumpet fanfares and worship. The moment comes when the priests are meant to offer sacrifices to the Lord and all of a sudden, unexpectedly, the presence of God fills the temple, so thick that it appears to people as a dense cloud. The moment this happens the priests are rendered helpless.

The New American Standard version of the Bible says that, *"The priests could not stand to minister because of the cloud"* (2 Chronicles 5:14). They literally fell on the floor and could not get up. They could not stand. Some people get upset when they see others fall over under the power of God, but here it is clearly in the Bible.

Read again the account of Jesus' arrest in the garden at Gethsemane in John chapter 18 and you will see an interesting detail that many people pass over:

> *"Judas, having received a detachment of troops, and officers from the chief priests and Pharisees, came there with lanterns, torches, and weapons. Jesus therefore, knowing all things that would come upon Him, went forward and said to them, 'Whom are you seeking?' They answered Him, 'Jesus of Nazareth.' Jesus said to*

them, 'I am He.' … Now when He said to them, 'I am He,'
they drew back and fell to the ground."

(John 18:3–6 NKJV)

We are familiar with the story: it was the middle of the night, Jesus had been praying in the garden, and His disciples had been falling asleep. All of a sudden a commotion breaks out as Judas, intent on betraying Jesus, arrives with the temple police and some troops. Jesus asks them who they are looking for and they tell Him, "Jesus of Nazareth." Jesus replies, "I am He" and they are literally driven backwards and fall to the ground. In fact, in the Greek, what Jesus literally said was, "I Am". In other words He described Himself in terms of the full weight of His divine nature.[2] At that moment the anointing of the Holy Spirit was felt so tangibly that these men were overwhelmed and fell backwards.

Some people might be surprised that such a thing could happen to a group of unbelievers. I don't believe that changes anything. The point is that a group of people with a will of their own, intent on arresting Jesus, were knocked down by the power of God. People get hung up on the "falling over" thing. I have even heard people say things like, "If you fall backwards it's not God. You fall on your face if

---

2. W. Hall Harris III, Professor of NT studies at Dallas Theological Seminary, in his commentary on John 5:18 says, "Jesus makes this affirmation of his identity using a formula which the reader has encountered before in the fourth Gospel, e.g., 8:24, 28, 58. Jesus has applied to himself the Divine Name of Exodus 3:14, 'I AM'. This amounts to something of a theophany which causes even his enemies to recoil and prostrate themselves, so that Jesus has to ask a second time, 'Whom are you seeking?' This is a vivid reminder that even in this dark hour, Jesus holds ultimate power over his enemies and the powers of darkness, because he is the One who bears the Divine Name." (*Source*: http://www.bible.org/page.php?page_id=2714)

it's God." Well, here we have examples of people falling both on their backs and face down, and in both instances it was clearly God at work. I think which way we fall when God overwhelms us is irrelevant. What is important to understand is that God has shown up!

Another interesting example of a human reaction to God's touch occurs in Acts chapter 10 where the writer of Acts recounts the incident where God speaks to Peter through a vision about the Gentiles being brought into the kingdom of God. Peter had gone up onto the roof of the house where he was staying so that he could pray quietly. The Bible says that he *"fell into a trance"* (Acts 10:10).

That is unusual language isn't it? To most people a "trance" sounds like a New Age or even occultish thing, but a trance is what happened to Peter. The Holy Spirit drew him into a waking vision. If you had been on that roof terrace with Peter, looking at him at that moment, you may have thought, "Peter was in prayer a moment ago, now his eyes have glazed over and he looks like he's staring at something!" Peter was. For a moment the world around him was dimmed down and his "reality" became the vision that God was placing before him. Afterwards you would want to ask him, "Peter, what just happened to you?" No doubt still stunned by what he had seen, he might have rambled a bit incoherently: "I saw a vision – a sheet came down from Heaven with all kinds of unclean foods in it. God said, 'Get up, kill and eat.' It happened three times and then it went away."

We need to put ourselves in Peter's shoes at this point and understand how much of a shake up this must have been for him. He went into a trance and was instructed by God to kill and eat things that were forbidden by the Law. But Peter was convinced it was God. If it happened today to a friend of ours, we would probably be highly skeptical. Most people's reaction would be, "If it contradicts Scripture then it's not God." That sounds like great advice to me, but it's not much use to Peter at this point. Peter is caught in a point of transition as God begins to move away from the Old Covenant of rules and regulations and unveils a New Covenant of grace and mercy based on a foundation of love. Because of that God is making a statement to Peter that does not make any biblical sense to him whatsoever.

I wonder what was in that sheet? Perhaps a pig, shrimp, crabs, reptiles? All we know is that it was forbidden food and that Peter was told he could eat it. The message from God was: *"Do not call anything impure that God has made clean"* (Acts 10:15). The next day the meaning of the vision was brought home to Peter and God confirmed His word as Peter visited the house of Cornelius the centurion and the Holy Spirit fell upon a group of Gentiles and they began speaking in tongues.

OTHER COMMON MANIFESTATIONS

There are numerous other manifestations that are common throughout Scripture. Here are just a few:

Shaking

"My legs gave way beneath me, and I shook in terror."
(HABAKKUK 3:16, NLT)

"The guards were so afraid of him that they shook and became like dead men."
(MATTHEW 28:4)

Laughing

"Abraham fell face down; he laughed..."
(GENESIS 17:17)

"Our mouths were filled with laughter,
*   our tongues with songs of joy . . . "*

(PSALM 126:2)

Shouting

"When the trumpets sounded, the people shouted, and at the
sound of the trumpet, when the people gave a loud shout, the wall
collapsed; so every man charged straight in, and they took the
city."

(JOSHUA 6:20)

In Joshua chapter 6 it was no ordinary shouting that was
taking place – there was a supernatural dimension to it and it
caused God's power to come. God Himself is recorded as
shouting by the prophet Isaiah:

"The LORD will march out like a mighty man,
*   like a warrior he will stir up his zeal;*
with a shout he will raise the battle cry
*   and will triumph over his enemies."*

(ISAIAH 42:13)

Speaking in tongues
Of all the manifestations listed in Scripture this is the one we
recognize the most because it is so closely associated with
being immersed in the Holy Spirit. There are numerous
scriptures that refer to it.

SOAKING IN THE PRESENCE OF GOD

When the revival broke out in Toronto in 1994 we really had
no precedent for the things we saw happening. People rarely
fell over in our meetings. I had seen it happen at Kathryn
Kuhlman meetings, but it happened very rarely when I

prayed for people. Then, in 1994, we began seeing multi-tudes of people fall under the power of God. It went from the occasional person falling over in a meeting every few years to hundreds falling over in a single meeting. And they didn't fall neatly in nice rows either – there were bodies strewn everywhere you looked.

We realized that we had a responsibility to try to pastor this phenomenon, so we tried to do all we could to ensure that people had room to lie down and that nobody got hurt. One thing that God made clear to us right from the beginning was that we shouldn't try to get people up or move them, we were to simply let them stay on the floor and "soak" in His presence, because that is where He would meet with them and minister to them.

We picked up the term "soaking" from Francis McNutt who had coined the phrase "soaking prayer", referring to a process of continual, persistent prayer for a person who needs to receive a healing touch from God. McNutt found that if he and his team prayed for people for prolonged periods of time, rather than praying short prayers over them, the increase in healings rose considerably. We too realized that when people go out under the power of God and stay there for as long as possible, just resting in His presence for an hour or more, all kinds of wonderful things would begin to happen in their lives. People would share stories about the fruit of their experience, how it affected them and what God had done for them.

The power of God is a reality, whether we understand it or not. Our God is an immense God! He spoke and the Universe came into existence. Scientists reckon that in our Milky Way galaxy there are around 100 billion stars. Our sun is one of the lesser of those stars. Here we are on this tiny blue planet in orbit around one of the lesser stars in the Milky Way, just one of countless other galaxies, and we think we know everything! We say things like, "Wait a minute, I can't believe in something unless I totally understand it." The fact is, we are never going to understand God! I spent a long time saying to the Lord,. "God, I don't understand. Why are you doing this?" I kept on telling God, "I don't understand ... I don't understand..." until finally God spoke to my heart and said, "John, you don't even understand women! Why would you think you'd understand Me?" "Wow!" I thought, "That is a very good point!" Why would I imagine that I could understand God? That helped me realize that I was just going to have to live with the fact that God will always do things I don't understand – and that's OK. I just have to trust Him and receive what He is doing by faith.

Why does that worry us so much? Because, legitimately, we don't want to fall into any kind of deception. No one wants to be deceived by a counterfeit. What can we do to ensure that doesn't happen? We need to read God's Word with an open and teachable spirit and ask Him to show us and confirm to us when something is really from Him. The more I witnessed things happening in Toronto, the more I went to God and prayed, "God, will you teach me? Will you show me what to do? Will you show me where this is in the Word? Will you confirm it to my heart?" I found that when I did that, He would speak to me and point out different passages of Scripture where I could find answers.

BUT WHY DO PEOPLE HAVE TO FALL DOWN?

Maybe you are still wondering, "Yes, but why do people have to fall down under God's power? What does it achieve?" I asked the Lord those very same questions and this is what I believe He said to me: "When people fall before Me two issues of the human heart are dealt with: fear and pride."

Fear says, "I don't want to be out of control. I don't want to leave my comfort zone because I don't know what might happen." Pride says, "I'm not doing that! I don't want to look a fool in front of everyone!" Both of these are attitudes of the heart that hinder us from experiencing the fullness of God's presence and are attitudes God wants us to live without. He doesn't want us to be afraid to surrender to Him and He doesn't want us to be full of pride either. Instead, He wants us to come to a place where we trust Him and can say, "God, whatever You want to do is cool with me." Jesus humbled Himself and subjected Himself to terrible humiliation so that we could be redeemed. What right then do we have to limit the way in which God works through us? People want to have God on their terms, but it doesn't work that way.

Fear also comes when people have been abused in the past and they fear being abused again. Their trust has been eroded and so it is difficult for them to come and make themselves vulnerable before God. But the Holy Spirit wants to teach all of us who are fearful that if we will just surrender to Him, He will tenderly take us to a place of rest in God's presence where healing can be poured out. We are safe in God's hands and He wants to help us conquer our fears.

WHAT IS THE FRUIT OF IT?

In as far as they go, manifestations are evidence of the fact that God is touching a person or that His presence is with us here and now. But what about after the falling over, laughing or crying? What is the lasting fruit of such experiences?

In late 1995 a Christian sociologist, Margaret Poloma, came to one of our meetings and told me she would like to interview a cross-section of people who had fallen under the power of the Spirit. At first I was a little worried about this, but I got to know Margaret and realized that she loved the Lord, so we decided, yes, let's have a survey and see what happened to those who are touched by God in this way.[3]

Margaret surveyed around 1,000 people as a representative sample. The sample contained a cross-section of people and each person had the opportunity to reflect on what had happened to them since God had touched them powerfully and they had soaked in His presence. The survey found that 92% of people testified to the fact that they were more in love with Jesus since the experience than they had ever been in their entire Christian life. The second most common result (with 82% of people mentioning it) was that they were more motivated and excited about sharing Jesus with family and friends than ever before.

In statistical terms, those are very high percentages to extrapolate from any sample group of people, so the survey proved to me that good fruit was resulting from the experiences people were having. People have often criticized the manifestations as being demonic, but loving Jesus more and wanting to tell others about Him doesn't sound like the devil's doing, does it? Nothing about the experiences of these people could be attributed to him, and not even to human emotionalism. You could argue that it was due to people getting carried away emotionally if nothing in their life subsequently changed, but this was not the case. If I had hazarded a guess beforehand, I would have said that maybe as many as 60% of people would have said, "I'm not sure what happened to me." But this was not the case. The overwhelming majority were very clear about the fact that they had been drawn so much closer to God.

---

3. You can read an extract from Margaret Poloma's survey in the Appendix of this book.

GOD VALUES CHILDLIKENESS

If we want to receive a fresh touch from God we must develop a childlike attitude that is expectant and willing to receive all that the Father has for us. Do you want more of God? I know I do! But the first requirement for receiving more of God's presence in our lives is to believe that He actually wants to bless us. Faith is a component of being touched by God – we have to believe! Often people watch from the sidelines as God touches others and they never press in themselves, simply because they don't believe that God would want to bless *them* in the same way. I have found the following Scripture really helpful in understanding how much God wants to bless His children:

"Which of you fathers, if your son asks for a fish, will give him a snake instead? Or if he asks for an egg, will give him a scorpion? If you then, though you are evil, know how to give good gifts to your children, how much more will your Father in heaven give the Holy Spirit to those who ask him!"

(LUKE 11:11–13)

Jesus pointed out to His listeners that, actually, God is nice! He is very, very kind. If, in an innocent, childlike way, we press in and ask Him for more, He's not going to say "no" because He is generous and wants to bless us abundantly. He knows how to give good gifts to His children and He's not at all reluctant to do it. For years I never realized how much fun God is. He loves childlikeness. We try to act so grown up and proper all the time and it doesn't help.

The fact that we have to adopt a childlike approach with God, coming to Him, making ourselves vulnerable, is another way in which the Father helps us to overcome our fear and pride. Pride says, "I can't humble myself and ask God for what I need." Fear says, "I can't make myself vulnerable – what if God rejects me?" I find it sad and wearying that the Body of Christ is so afraid of pressing into God. Instead of receiving like little children we act so sophisticated as we worry about falling into deception or being taken in by a counterfeit experience of God. I believe the enemy has used that lie to keep hundreds of thousands of Christians from receiving the blessing of God on their lives. An overbearing fear of deception can cause us to miss God's blessing.

What I find most amazing is the fact that people give the devil so much credit. They seem to think he can come and do anything he likes and that somehow God can't! I want people to have more faith in God's ability to bless them than in the devil's ability to deceive them. God is greater!

Jesus affirmed the need for childlikeness in His ministry and emphasized the basic simplicity of our relationship with the Father. In Luke chapter 10 we read of His reaction when the seventy-two disciples He sent out come to report back to Him. Luke 10:17 says,

"The seventy-two returned with joy and said, 'Lord, even the demons submit to us in your name.'"

Jesus responds with these well known words:

"... do not rejoice that the spirits submit to you, but rejoice that your names are written in heaven."

(LUKE 10:20)

Then we read that Jesus began rejoicing and talking privately with the Father and tells Him,

"... I praise you, Father, Lord of heaven and earth, because you have hidden theses things from the wise and learned, and revealed

them to little children. Yes, Father, for this was your good pleasure."

(LUKE 10:21)

Incidentally, did you realize that this is one occasion in Scripture where Jesus Himself was overcome by the power of God? The first part of verse 21, preceding Jesus' comment, says, *"At that time Jesus, full of joy through the Holy Spirit, said…"* The Contemporary English Version renders the verse this way: *"Jesus felt the joy that comes from the Holy Spirit."* He was overcome with God's goodness. Inexpressible joy was bubbling up within Him and overflowing.

But what really strikes me about this verse is the fact that Jesus rejoices over the fact that God's kingdom is hidden from a large number of people. What kind of evangelist gets excited about the fact that his message is hidden from a group of people? Yet, here is Jesus, exuberant about the fact! What He is really saying, of course, is, that those with childlike simplicity are able to "get" this, whilst those who think they're so smart will, in their smugness, "miss" it. Thinking we've got God all figured out is just another form of pride. God wants to surround Himself with little children who just want a relationship with Him – those who will enter into His presence and be overwhelmed by it. God places a high value on such humility. Do you value childlikeness? We should, even if our whole lives people have constantly told us to grow up!

Elsewhere Jesus said that unless we become like little children we cannot even enter the kingdom of God (Luke 18:17). Why? Because a characteristic of childlikeness is trust and innocence. We have to have a fundamental trust in God in order to be able to enter in.

Given the fact that God so affirms childlikeness, isn't it reasonable to think that people who are being touched by the power of God might act in a childlike way? We have seen people filled with the joy of the Holy Spirit laugh, roll around on the floor and run about, just like children. They get so overwhelmed with joy that they don't know what to do with themselves. This may appear to be "childish" to others, but we shouldn't judge what God may be doing in their hearts.

Did anyone act in a childlike way in the Bible? Yes. One of the best examples is King David, a man who had an exceptionally intimate relationship with the God. David was so overcome with the joy of the Lord that he danced in the street in his underwear! And his wife wasn't amused by this. She was full of scorn for David and said it was entirely inappropriate for someone in his position to be doing such a thing. David's response was simply, *"I will become even more undignified than this, and I will be humiliated in my own eyes"* (2 Samuel 6:22). This is the secret of childlike faith: take your eyes off yourself and focus them on the Father.

THE ISSUE OF SELF-CONTROL

Some people will ask, what about self-control? Isn't that a fruit of the Spirit? So why would people being touched by God show so little self-restraint? Whilst I totally agree with the need for self-control and would want to pastor any uncontrolled, carnal behavior in the context of a public meeting, I have to look at the evidence of Scripture and see that often God moves upon a person in such a way that they have little choice in how to respond.

Take, for example, the conversion of the apostle Paul. Saul, as he was formerly known, was an angry young man, very zealous and sincere about his religion, but sincerely wrong. He was busy persecuting Christians when he has an astonishing encounter with Jesus on the road.

"As he neared Damascus on his journey, suddenly a light from heaven flashed around him. He fell to the ground and heard a voice say to him, 'Saul, Saul, why do you persecute me?'

'Who are you Lord?' Saul asked.
'I am Jesus, whom you are persecuting,' he replied. 'Now get
up and go into the city, and you will be told what you must do.' "

(ACTS 9:3–6)

When Saul got up he was blind. He couldn't see a thing. What must his friends have thought? "What on earth just happened to Saul?" The experience must have knocked the wind out of him. "Jesus, the one I've been persecuting, just appeared and spoke to me!" Saul must have been turning his thoughts over and over as he traveled back to the city, wondering what was going to happen next. Saul was apprehended by God, overwhelmed by His presence, and there was nothing he could do about it. He was so stubborn in his beliefs that it seems God had no other way of getting through to him. But God had a destiny for his life that He was determined would be fulfilled.

I ask the question again, what if you witnessed something like this yourself as a casual observer? You see a guy fall to the ground under the power of God and when he gets back up again he's blind! That doesn't sound right, does it? What kind of God would blind a guy? It can't be Jesus, surely? It must be the devil. Can you see how preconditioned our thinking is? How easily we ascribe supernatural, out-of-the-box events to the devil, but not to God? What if you are a pastor and this happens to someone during your Sunday morning service. A young guy comes into the meeting. He's not a Christian, in fact, he's anti-Christian, an outspoken and militant atheist. No one expects him to be touched by the worship or the sermon, but the next thing you know, the power of God has hit him and he's on the floor. He gets up and it's obvious he has met with God, but he can't see.

Imagine taking a phone call from that guy's mother the next morning! She wants to know what kind of church you're running over there and what you've done to her son.

asked by the Pharisees, "Which is the greatest command-
ment in the Law?" He responded by saying,

> " 'Love the Lord your God with all your heart and with all your
> soul and with all your mind.' This is the first and greatest
> commandment. And the second is like it: 'Love your neighbor as
> yourself.' All the Law and the Prophets hang on these two
> commandments."
>
> (MATTHEW 22:37–40)

Notice that we are not just called to love God mentally, with
our minds. Our emotions are involved too – our hearts and
souls. The Bible begins and ends with a marriage. Jesus
wants a Bride who loves Him. He doesn't merely want a
working Bride or a serving Bride or a theologically correct
Bride. That is important, but He wants a Bride that not only
serves Him but loves Him; one that is full of emotion and
passion, a Bride that just cannot live without Him. God
wants to persuade all those who have developed a rational
brand of Christianity that as good as that is, there is more!
We can also enjoy and engage with the Father emotionally
and when God touches us by His power it is right that our
emotions play their part.

PRACTICAL ADVICE
FOR PASTORS/LEADERS

To end this section on a very practical note, many pastors
and leaders have asked me how to pastor situations where
people are experiencing the power of God and reacting in
different ways. Whilst there are no hard and fast rules,
experience has taught me that there can be a connection
between a person's reaction and what God is doing in their
heart. No advice can replace asking God for discernment
and spiritual insight into individual situations, but I hope the

following general guidelines are helpful. Here are five different scenarios:

Imagine it's Sunday morning in your church. You have invited the Holy Spirit to come and do what He wants in the meeting and He has shown up in power. People are falling down and there is laughing, crying, groaning, shouting. You notice the best givers in your church standing on the other side of the room with their arms folded and a look on their faces that says, "If you don't deal with this now, we're out that door and you'll never see us again!" So you want to make sure this is of God!

Person #1

The first person you investigate is contorting their face and you think, "This looks demonic to me." You need to ask yourself, are the demons coming or going? If you believe they are going they you can simply pray, "More, Lord." Remember that things like this happened frequently during Jesus' ministry. If you make the rule "no screaming in my church" then Jesus might not visit that often – it happened all the time wherever He went.

We can also pray that the Holy Spirit comes and drives out everything the Father wants out (such as fear, shame anger and the demonic) and brings in everything the Father wants in (love, joy, peace, power and boldness).

Person #2

The second person you see is laughing and crying alternatively. Is this good or is it bad? What's happening to them? First of all, don't be afraid to speak to them and ask them. People under the power of the Spirit haven't "checked out", it's just that the reality of this world has been dimmed down a bit and the reality of the unseen world has been magnified. They can still connect with you, so ask them, "How are you? Is everything OK? What's going on?" They may tell you: "God is dealing with some really deep hurts from my past and showing me He was there with me when it happened and it's going to be OK." When people suddenly realize how much bigger God is than all of their problems, it can often strike them as being incredibly funny and that's when the laughter starts. Many people have testified to the fact that they laughed and laughed until they realized God had dealt with the issue that was bothering them. Others have just needed to cry before God, weep before Him, and the heavy burden of their hurts has been shed along with the tears.

Person #3

The next person is just laughing. My friend, Peter Jackson, when the power of God fell on him in early 1994, began laughing and he is still laughing now, fifteen years later! He just laughs and laughs. I thought he was going to laugh himself to death, but he didn't, and it was good. Ask that person, "What's going on with you?" and they may respond, "Oh, I just have these waves of glory coming over me. I feel like if one more wave comes over me I'll explode and that'll be the end of me."

I personally had a similar experience way back in the mid-seventies, where waves of glory washed over me and I felt as if I might not live through it. Then, in February 1994, just a few weeks into the revival in Toronto, I had another similar experience.

Carol and I were speaking at a seminar in the nearby city of Hamilton. The Holy Spirit fell on us all at that meeting and we had an amazing time. One night, just as we were leaving, a little girl came up to us and prophesied over me. The extraordinary thing was that she did it in perfect rhyme. All the while I was thinking, "How can she do that? It's amazing!" but it had a dramatic effect on me and I fell to the floor. Eventually I collected myself and we made our way outside to our car.

For some reason the remote central locking wasn't working so I was trying to get the car key into the door lock and I just couldn't do it. Then I began laughing and laughing. I remember thinking several things as I stood there laughing at nearly 1.00 am in the morning. First of all, I was thinking, "I'm laughing so loud and yet nothing's funny! What am I laughing at?" The second thing was, "My mouth is open so wide. It's not how I would normally laugh." Finally, we got in the car and went to McDonalds for a coffee. No sooner had I walked in there than it all hit me again!

One could reasonably ask, what was all that about? The fact is, I don't know, but it was fun! It was childlike and the love of God was so near, so real, the joy of the Lord so explosive. The peace of God that came after it was amazing – I didn't have a care in the world.

So if a person is laughing, that's a good thing. I remember in the early days that many people were disgusted by the laughter: "Isn't it terrible, people laughing in church" etc. People are a bit more used to it now. Yet why should people be offended by laughter? Medical studies have shown that laughter is very therapeutic. Laughter is like medicine (Proverbs 17:22), it releases endorphins into the brain and brings a sense of wellbeing and wholeness. So when the Holy Spirit comes and causes you to laugh He knows what you need, so just let Him do it. How do you know if it's of God? Because of the fruit of the Spirit that results. Remember, don't make a judgment based on a snapshot, but look for the long-term fruit. If it draws that person closer to Jesus, then it's good.

Person #4
You see a fourth person who is just being hysterical and you think, "Hmm, I don't know about this. Maybe this person is faking it." Why would you think that? Perhaps because you're their pastor, you've known them a long time and

there is a little bit of history there. Or perhaps because you've had a bit of experience and you can tell the real thing, compared to someone who is manufacturing it.

Why would someone fake it? Because there are sincere people who want to enter in and don't know how, who think that if they act like everyone else is acting then they'll get what everyone else is getting. Unfortunately, it doesn't work like that. That's a bit like a group of people congregating in a sports stadium, figuring that if they shout and cheer loud enough, maybe some teams will turn up and they'll have a game going. It's putting the cart before the horse.

So you can lovingly say to any person who seems to be trying too hard, "Come on now, take it easy, just wait. We'll pray for you. We'll ask the Holy Spirit to come and touch you. God has something real for you, you don't have to make this up."

We need to understand that with the things of the Spirit we are on our honor. We don't need to put on anything. When God touches us for real, often it is so intense that we will be begging Him to stop! But we don't need to fake it. Sometimes people will put it on because they want to feel accepted as part of a group and don't want to be left out. As a pastor, don't beat people up over this, but encourage them to wait for the real thing.

Person #5

A final type of manifestation one might encounter is when the person is not only responding emotionally to the power of God, but the Holy Spirit is orchestrating something with them i.e. they are responding physically, usually acting as a type of prophetic message to others. It is this type of manifestation that has given us the most trouble from our critics and, to that end, the next section of the book is devoted to helping the reader understand more about the subject of prophetic symbolism.

PART 2

THE IMPORTANCE OF PROPHETIC SYMBOLISM

Immediately after Pentecost, when the Holy Spirit was moving in power like never before, a great revival broke out that swept over the entire Greek Roman empire. In a very short time there were countless conversions to Christ as the kingdom of God expanded. But the burgeoning Church had strong leaders in place – Matthew, Mark, Luke, John, Peter – who were apostles, prophets, evangelists, pastors and teachers, and these God-appointed men acted like "banks" to the river that was flowing. Every move of the Spirit needs to be pastored in a responsible way. Even though the Spirit of God was moving powerfully and rapidly to establish the early Church, there wasn't just holy chaos; the move of God was pastored by these men who were teachable and accountable, both to the Lord and to one another.

As the revival in Toronto gained impetus, I was committed to give pastoral oversight, but I was not always sure how to do it and often feeling quite overwhelmed. One day I was talking to the Lord about this and said, "Lord, what do I do? I don't know where to start. What things I should leave alone and what things I should put a stop to?" Amazingly, God just replied with just one word and this has been the greatest help to me ever since: "Ask!"

That single word launched me on a journey of listening closely to God and asking for His discernment regarding every situation I encountered. Sometimes I would ask Him, "What about this, Lord?" and He would say, "I'm not comfortable with that. Why don't you ask that person to stop?" At other times I would ask the same question and He would say, "This is Me at work. Let it go."

Leaders need to keep close to God and to operate in spiritual discernment at all times. Every situation in church life needs pastoring, not in a heavy-handed way, but as the Holy Spirit directs. Even our prayer meetings, for example, need that kind of attention. What could be wrong with praying? one might ask. Well, if one person is dominating the prayer meeting with their agenda and others are not getting the opportunity to pray, that needs to be gently addressed. Another example would be dancing as an expression of worship. Mostly it will be fine, but not if someone chooses to jump onto the platform waving an enormous flag! That would just draw attention to them instead of the Lord!

We need to give pastoral oversight that is full of love, full of faith, willing to take risks, desiring God to move, but at the same time willing to deal with things that are out of order. I feel we have been very blessed in Toronto to have had only a handful of incidents where people were unwilling to accept our correction when they were out of line. But out of over four million visitors who have come through our doors I think that's pretty amazing. God makes a way whenever we make a decision to remain loving, childlike and dependent upon Him.

PROPHETIC SYMBOLISM

I have often been asked about one particular type of manifestation that occurs in our meetings, which I describe as "prophetic symbolism". Why do people sometimes behave in an unusual way as if acting something out? What does it mean? This section of the book is dedicated to examining this biblical manifestation of the Spirit, showing how frequently it occurs in Scripture, and looks at how we should respond to it.

My journey to understanding this phenomenon began with my wife, Carol. I think God allowed this in His providence so that I would not be quick to dismiss it as wacky or extreme. It taught me that, sometimes, under the power of the Spirit people are communicating something through their actions, rather than merely responding emotionally to God's touch.

On this occasion, God's Spirit was moving powerfully and Carol was being touched. She looked to me as though she was flying like an eagle. Her arms were spread out wide and at times she was gliding, at other times flapping her arms like wings. I didn't know what was going on but I felt to leave her. Speaking to her later I asked her what had happened and discovered that she had experienced an incredible waking vision. From an aerial viewpoint, soaring with the Holy Spirit, she saw a crown hovering over Europe and fire coming out of the crown engulfing England and moving across the English Channel to spread into the surrounding European nations. That vision became the basis of a vitally important word from God for our European friends and partners. I thought to myself, "What if, through fear of emotionalism and getting carried away, I had put a stop to this?" I realized then that I could easily have shut down something that was clearly from God.

A similar thing happened on another occasion when Carol and I traveled to Stirling in Scotland to speak at a gathering of pastors. I remember it clearly because these pastors had come together to "check out" this guy from Toronto and to see if all they had been hearing about was really from God. A young lady from Ireland called Liz was there to lead the worship for the event. Liz led the worship beautifully; the praise and worship were awesome and she took us into God's presence. The only problem was, every now and then, without warning, she would crow like a rooster! Inwardly I thought, "Oh no. Of all the times, in a pastor's meeting we have to deal with this! What am I going to say?"

I can't recall exactly what I did say, but somehow I fudged my way through and made some excuse for what was happening. Later I asked Liz what was going on and why she was crowing from time to time (which I learned is what you must always do: just ask the person, "What are you sensing, what do you feel God is saying?"). She replied, "I feel like the Lord is saying, 'Church, it's time to wake up! There's a new day coming. It's time to wake up.'" Although the prophetic symbolism took people by surprise, including me, the message was entirely appropriate. I believe God sometimes does things like this intentionally to see who is trying to approach Him cerebrally and who is prepared to come to Him like a little child, ready to hear what He has to say.

Throughout Scripture God shows Himself to us as the God who is primarily interested in our hearts. More than anything He wants to know if we are "on board" with Him, fully committed. There are numerous scriptures that talk about the heart, but one of my favorites is found in Luke chapter 2 where Mary and Joseph take Jesus to be dedicated in the temple. Simeon, a prophet, takes the baby Jesus in his arms and speaks some amazing things over Him:

> *"Sovereign Lord, as you have promised,*
> * you now dismiss your servant in peace.*
> *For my eyes have seen your salvation,*
> * which you have prepared in the sight of all people,*
> *a light for revelation to the Gentiles*
> * and for glory to your people Israel."*
>
> (LUKE 2:29–32)

Imagine Mary and Joseph's reaction – they must have been shocked by this confirmation of Jesus' purpose and destiny. But there is more: Simeon goes on to say,

> *"This child is destined to cause the falling and rising of many in Israel, and to be a sign that will be spoken against, so that the thoughts of many hearts will be revealed."*
>
> (LUKE 2:34 –35)

How could the Messiah be the cause of many falling away? A sign that will be spoken against? The most important thing to God is that our hearts are revealed. God wants us to be connected to Him at a deep level. He wants to capture our heart. The religious authorities never understood what was happening with Jesus because of both their misconceptions about the Messiah and because they never allowed God to capture their hearts. Jesus was a stumbling stone to them because the truths of God's kingdom are revealed to little children and hidden from the wise and learned.

We have to approach prophetic symbolism with the same attitude – to look beyond merely attempting to rationalize it, and to look for the heart and message of God in it.

In 1998, when Microsoft was introducing Windows 98, they heralded its arrival with a TV commercial that showed a barnyard scene. A rooster flew up onto a fence and crowed away, "Cock-a-doodle-do," then the tag line appeared: "It's a new day!" No one was offended or angry at Microsoft for producing a stupid or insulting commercial. But transfer that into the Church, with our friend Liz crowing like a rooster to say, "Wake up, Church, it's a new day!" and suddenly everyone is offended, insulted and angry about it. But this is often the way when God moves. Those with ears to hear will grasp it immediately, whilst others will struggle. Paul makes this point in 1 Corinthians 2.

In 1 Corinthians 2:4–5 he tells his readers,

"My message and my preaching were not with wise and persuasive words, but with a demonstration of the Spirit's power, so that your faith might not rest on men's wisdom, but on God's power."

Later, in verse 14, he backs up his comments with:

"People who aren't spiritual can't receive these truths from God's Spirit. It all sounds foolish to them and they can't understand it, for only those who are spiritual can understand what the Spirit means."

(NLT)

The thinking, rational mind struggles to understand the things of the Spirit because they seem like foolishness. Therefore, when we see something that appears strange to us, we need to be slow to pass judgment and use the discernment the Holy Spirit provides.

Consider the comment of Jesus in Luke 10:1–21 at the end of the story about the seventy-two disciples who, returning from ministering with great joy, said, *"Lord, even the demons submit to us in your name."* Verse 21 says,

"At that very time He rejoiced greatly in the Holy Spirit, and said, 'I praise You, O Father, Lord of heaven and earth, that You have hidden these things from the wise and intelligent and have revealed them to infants. Yes, Father, for this way was well-pleasing in Your sight.'"

(NASB)

Sometimes the direct intention of God is to hide His mysteries from the "wise and learned" and yet reveal them to the trusting hearts of the childlike. This is the very same reason Jesus usually spoke to them in parables.

"The disciples came to him and asked, 'Why do you speak to the people in parables?'

He replied, 'The knowledge of the secrets of the kingdom of heaven has been given to you, but not to them. Whoever has will be given more, and he will have an abundance. Whoever does not have, even what he has will be taken from him. This is why I speak to them in parables:

'Though seeing, they do not see;
though hearing, they do not hear or understand.

In them is fulfilled the prophecy of Isaiah:

"You will be ever hearing but never understanding;
you will be ever seeing but never perceiving.
For this people's heart has become calloused;
they hardly hear with their ears,
and they have closed their eyes.

Otherwise they might see with their eyes,
*   hear with their ears,*
*   understand with their hearts*
and turn, and I would heal them."

But blessed are your eyes because they see, and your ears because
they hear. For I tell you the truth, many prophets and righteous
men longed to see what you see but did not see it, and to hear what
you hear but did not hear it.' "

(MATTHEW 13:10–17)

EXAMPLES OF PROPHETIC SYMBOLISM IN SCRIPTURE

When God speaks He often speaks in the language of dreams and visions, symbols and mysteries. When you think about it, all language is rooted in symbolism. If I were to say to you the word "car" you would immediately picture something in your mind, perhaps your own car, a friend's car etc. If I were to say "father" or "mother" to you, those words would also create instant images in your mind. Pictures and language are closely related. In fact, the basis of the earliest languages was graphical, such as Egyptian hieroglyphs or Chinese characters which represent whole phrases or concepts.

Similarly, the Bible uses a vast array of imagery to convey its message to us and is rich with symbolism. Reading it one cannot help but be struck by the constant use of imagery, typology and symbolism to convey deep spiritual truths and to foreshadow future events. Let's look at some examples:

The Passover lamb
The Bible refers to Jesus as, *"the Lamb who was slain from the foundation of the world."* The Lamb of God is a prophetic symbol that is clearly seen throughout the entire span of Scripture. Nowhere is it more poignant than when the

people of God are instructed to kill the Passover lamb on the eve of their Exodus from Egypt (Exodus chapter 12).

Here God told Moses to instruct the people to take a one-year old lamb that was pure, faultless and spotless; to kill it and put the blood on the doorposts of their houses. Then, when the Lord passed through the land striking down every firstborn man and animal, when He saw the blood He would pass over that household.

This was an awesome, symbolic picture of the day that was coming when Jesus, the true Lamb of God, would die on a cross for the sins of the whole world. The judgment of God's wrath passes over all those who have identified themselves with His blood by applying it to the doorposts of their heart.

What would have happened if the people had not performed this symbolic act? If someone had said, "I'm not doing that. I'm not killing a lamb and putting its blood on our door"? Their firstborn would have died along with the Egyptians because they didn't honor the prophetic, symbolic act that God was asking them to perform. The Jewish people, to this day, celebrate Passover, but would not identify with this aspect of its symbolism, not recognizing or believing that it points to Christ and His sacrifice.

This theme is repeated many times in Scripture. In Genesis we read that, because of their sin, Adam and Eve covered themselves with leaves. But their leaves were not good enough. So God taught them how to cover themselves properly with animal skins. But where did those skins come from? An animal had to be sacrificed. Blood was shed in order for Adam and Eve to be "covered". It is yet another picture of the sacrificial Lamb of God.

Moses and the water
Often, like the act of preparing the Passover lamb, prophetic symbols have to be acted out to underline their significance.

In Exodus chapter 17 we read about one such instance, where Moses performs a prophetic act in front of the people of God. They have been trekking through the desert wilderness and all the people are thirsty, having been without water for something like three days. The people are complaining bitterly: *"Why did you bring us up out of Egypt to make us and our children and livestock die of thirst?"* (Exodus 17:3). Moses cries out to God for help, saying, *"What am I to do with these people? They are almost ready to stone me"* (verse 4). So God speaks to Moses and instructs him to perform a specific act:

> *" 'Walk on ahead of the people. Take with you some of the elders of Israel and take in your hand the staff with which you struck the Nile, and go. I will stand there before you by the rock at Horeb. Strike the rock, and water will come out of it for the people to drink.' So Moses did this in the sight of the elders of Israel."*
>
> (Exodus 17:5–6)

Moses was in a tight spot. If you wander around in the desert for a few days and don't find water then you are in serious trouble. No one can survive for long in that environment, so there was a real risk here. God tells Moses to hit a rock with his stick. If Moses had been the kind of person that Paul described in 1 Corinthians 2:14, he might have said, "Come on God, you don't get water by hitting a rock with a stick! Everyone knows that. You get water by digging a well, so show us where to dig!"

> *"The man without the Spirit does not accept the things that come from the Spirit of God, for they are foolishness to him, and he cannot understand them, because they are spiritually discerned."*
>
> (1 Corinthians 2:14)

But Moses understands that God often speaks symbolically and uses prophetic symbols to accomplish His purposes, so he strikes the rock with his stick and water gushes out. Think about that – it had to be a flood of water because it needed to serve some 2.5 million people and their livestock. It wasn't just a little stream, but a lot of water! Moses got the miracle because he cooperated with God's method.

Some time later, however, Moses finds himself in the same predicament. Numbers chapter 20 outlines a similar scenario: the Israelite community arrive at the Desert of Zin and are camped at Kadesh. We read that, *"... there was no water for the community, and the people gathered in opposition to Moses and Aaron ...* [the people said] *'Why did you bring us up out of Egypt to this terrible place?'"* (verses 2, 5). Once again Moses asks for God's help and this time the Lord gives him a different instruction:

> *"Take the staff, and you and your brother Aaron gather the assembly together. Speak to that rock before their eyes and it will pour out its water. You will bring water out of the rock for the community so they and their livestock can drink."*
>
> (NUMBERS 20:8)

This time Moses has to speak to the rock rather than strike it. Again, spiritual things must be spiritually discerned. Speaking to a rock to make it produce water is just foolishness to the natural mind.

Moses knows God's supernatural ways better than anyone, but something else is introduced into this situation: anger. Moses is fed up with the people's constant complaining and their blaming him for everything and he is mad, so he says,

> *" 'Listen, you rebels, must we bring you water out of this rock?' Then Moses raised his arm and struck the rock twice with his staff. Water gushed out, and the community and their livestock drank."*
>
> (NUMBERS 20:10–11)

What is interesting here is that although Moses did not obey the letter of God's command the water still arrived – a demonstration of God's grace. But because Moses lost his temper and dishonored God publicly he got himself into serious trouble.

> *"The LORD said to Moses and Aaron, 'Because you did not trust in me enough to honor me as holy in the sight of the Israelites, you will not bring this community into the land I give them.'"*
>
> (NUMBERS 20:12)

In our private devotions my wife, Carol, would always feel bad for Moses. Poor Moses! Because of his disobedience in this one situation he was disqualified from leading the people into the Promised Land. If he can get into trouble for hitting a rock instead of speaking to it, what hope is there for you and me?

But in this instance Moses violated a very important symbolic picture! What is the prophetic symbolism at work here? The rock is a type of Christ and the stick is a type of the cross. Jesus Christ was stricken with the cross and living water came gushing out to water a human race that was dying of spiritual thirst. But Christ can never be crucified again. After that once-for-all sacrifice we only need to speak and ask for living water.

Moses violated a very important prophetic symbol that God was using to foreshadow what His Son would accomplish. Moses, at that moment, was a prophetic type himself, representing the Law. The Law is always too hard, too severe. We are desperately in need of the grace that comes through Jesus because no one can perfectly keep the Law. The Law existed to prove to us that no matter how good a person is, they are never good enough. We all need a Savior.

The death of Elisha

We read about another interesting symbolic prophetic act in 2 Kings 13 at the time of the death of the prophet Elisha. Verse 14 says,

"When Elisha became sick with the illness of which he was to die, Jehoash the king of Israel came down to him and wept over him and said, 'My father, my father, the chariots of Israel and its horsemen!' "

(NASB)

Jehoash is reiterating the words Elisha himself spoke when his mentor, Elijah, was taken away. The man of God is about to depart and the king laments, "What are we going to do now?"

Elisha instructs the king to get a bow and some arrows. Elisha tells the king, "Put your hand on the bow", so he takes it up. Then Elisha put his hands on the king's hand as if imparting an anointing. He asks for a window facing towards the east to be opened and then he cries out, "Shoot!" What is happening here? It is more than just the shooting of an arrow. This act has spiritual significance and meaning. The arrow flies out of the window and strikes the ground outside. Then Elisha pronounces,

"The LORD's arrow of victory, even the arrow of victory over Aram; for you will defeat the Arameans at Aphek until you have destroyed them."

(2 KINGS 13:17, NASB)

Elisha had a prophetic proclamation to make and the act of firing the arrow was an integral part of it. This arrow became the arrow of the Lord's deliverance, a symbol representing the fact that God would act on behalf of His people to rout their enemies. Elisha then had further instructions for Jehoash:

> *"Then he said, 'Take the arrows,' and the king took them.*
> *Elisha told him, 'Strike the ground.' He struck it three times*
> *and stopped. The man of God was angry with him and said,*
> *'You should have struck the ground five or six times; then you*
> *would have defeated Aram and completely destroyed it. But now*
> *you will defeat it only three times.' "*
>
> (2 KINGS 13:18–19)

I don't picture Jehoash taking a handful of arrows and hitting the floor: boom, boom, boom. He is shooting them out of the window, one after another, and they are striking the ground outside. He shoots two more arrows and then stops, but the man of God is angry with him. "Didn't you hear what I said?" Elisha asks. "Didn't you hear the prophetic proclamation? This is the arrow of the Lord's deliverance; you should have shot five or six times, then you would have completely defeated the Arameans. But because you only did it three times, you'll only win three battles."

The implication is that more arrows were available to the king than he used. There were perhaps half a dozen arrows left after he shot the first one and he should have used them all, cooperating with the prophetic symbol to obtain a comprehensive victory over the enemies of God's people. Verse 25 confirms that Jehoash did in fact only accomplish three victories against his enemies.

This is a clear example of the fact that obedience to prophetic symbolism can release tremendous blessing. In this case, disobedience changed the course of history.

What about in the New Testament?

Jesus and the fig tree
Mark's Gospel chapter 11 recounts a story from the last week in Jesus' life on earth. Jesus and His disciples are leaving Bethany on their way to Jerusalem and Jesus is

hungry. He sees a fig tree in the distance and goes to see if He can find something to eat from it. The Bible tells us,

> *"When he reached it, he found nothing but leaves, because it was not the season for figs. Then he said to the tree, 'May no one ever eat fruit from you again.' And his disciples heard him say it."*
> (MARK 11:13–14)

Skipping on to verse 20 we read that,

> *"In the morning, as they went along, they saw the fig tree withered from the roots. Peter remembered and said to Jesus, 'Rabbi, look! The fig tree you cursed has withered!'*
> *'Have faith in God,' Jesus answered."*
> (MARK 11:20–22)

Nothing Jesus did was ever done randomly, for no reason. Everything He did had a purpose. It is significant in this story that the Bible says "it was not the season for figs". Jesus must have known this only too well, so it is clear His act had a much deeper significance. The fig tree is a type of the nation of Israel and the Old Covenant.[4] Jesus, only days later, would face the cross and transition mankind from the Old Covenant of works into the New Covenant of grace.

---

4. Matthew Henry's commentary: **Verses 12–18** – Christ looked to find some fruit, for the time of gathering figs, though it was near, was not yet come; but he found none. He made this fig-tree an example, not to the trees, but to the men of that generation. It was a figure of the doom upon the Jewish church, to which he came seeking fruit, but found none. Christ went to the temple, and began to reform the abuses in its courts, to show that when the Redeemer came to Zion, it was to turn away ungodliness from Jacob. The scribes and the chief priests sought, not how they might make their peace with him, but how they might destroy him. A desperate attempt, which they could not but fear was fighting against God.

Prophetically, He went to the Old Covenant looking for fruit and found nothing, so He made the final proclamation, "May no one eat fruit from you ever again" and the fig tree shriveled up. Now, since the cross, no one can be saved through works by keeping the Law; salvation comes only by grace through faith in Christ. The fig tree was a powerful picture of transition. It is no longer works of righteousness that we have done, but by faith in Christ alone do we find peace with God.

Anecdotal examples

There are numerous other biblical examples one could quote, but there has also been powerful anecdotal evidence of the importance of prophetic symbolism. Here are a few examples.

On one occasion, when I was away from Toronto traveling with Randy Clark, I called the church to speak to a member of staff and ask how everything was going. The lady I spoke to was upbeat and said, "Everything is going great. By the way, last night we had a guy in the meeting who was roaring like a lion." Immediately, I was concerned. "What?" I said. "Oh yeah," she replied, "he was really roaring." "I hope you took him out of the meeting and prayed for deliverance," I responded. "No," she said. "We thought it was God." I wasn't sure about this at all.

When I returned home the person in question was still around so I had the opportunity to speak to him and ask him what had happened. His name was Gideon, a leader of leaders in the Chinese Christian community and very well respected. I thought to begin with that our staff member must have gotten mixed up because he seemed fine to me. In fact, I let him get up and share in the next meeting how he had come to Toronto fasting and praying and how God had told him, "Stop fasting, this is a feast. Eat, drink and enjoy it."

But, in the middle of giving his testimony in front of everyone, he began roaring like a lion again and even lunging towards the front row. I was just stunned. "What is he doing?" I thought. "What's going on?" Then he stopped roaring and spoke: "Do you know, for thousands of years my Chinese people have been absolutely destroyed by the power of the dragon. But now the Lion of the tribe of Judah is going to crush him!"

At that point everyone in the meeting cheered and whooped! They knew right away that it was God moving upon Gideon; it was such a powerful moment.

Scientists say that people will remember about 20% of what they hear, but 80% of what they *see* and hear. Obviously God knows this. The result of Gideon's actions combined with his words meant that this is a prophecy that I will remember till the day I die. If he had stood up and said, "Thus saith the Lord, 'The Lion of Judah is going to crush the dragon over China.'" We'd have all said, "Amen, brother." We would all have agreed that it was a good word, but would probably have forgotten about it soon afterwards. It got our attention because the word was acted out and demonstrated before our eyes.

Another time, near the beginning of the revival, Carol was overwhelmed by the Holy Spirit and was lying on the platform laughing. Every now and again she would wave her arms and legs about and laugh even more. She was even "running" on her back with her legs up in the air. I appreciate that many people may have been puzzled about what was going on and thinking, "Why doesn't he get his wife off the platform? She's distracting everyone doing all these antics . . . " but I felt God say to leave her. I knew that Carol, by temperament, isn't the type of person to put on a show for people.

Soon after Carol told me that she had just had an amazing vision. She found herself in Heaven with Jesus, playing with

Him in a field, dancing together. Then she went into a great banqueting hall and could see tables laid out as far as the eye could see. The Lord was saying to her, "I want you to get up and tell the people that the banquet feast is almost prepared and they are to be like the five wise virgins – buy oil!"

We know the story: Jesus told the parable in Matthew chapter 25 about five virgins who were wise and five who were foolish. The word God gave us through Carol was about the importance of spending time in His presence to get extra "oil", the oil of the Holy Spirit, as we soak in His anointing. Some think that lying on the floor just soaking is a waste of time, but no, you are receiving extra oil.

At the time I thought, "Wow, that's a beautiful admonishing word" and that was the end of it. Later, however, when God gave me more revelation about prophetic symbolism, I realized again that had I put a stop to what Carol was doing, move her off the platform, I would have shut down the word of the Lord to us. Receiving in His presence became a very important way in which God would move in people's lives over the coming years. If we had not made room for this word to be shared then the revival would probably have lasted for all of three weeks.

When the Holy Spirit orchestrates a prophetic statement through a person's actions something very powerful occurs. We must learn to pay attention to what the Holy Spirit is saying and doing and exercise discernment when people are acting under His power. They could be demonstrating a powerful word that God wants us to hear. We need to be led by the Spirit and remember to be childlike, but not childish, in approaching the things of the Spirit. Let God be God. "Prove all things and hold fast to that which is good."

HARD TO
RECEIVE?

Over the years we have heard the testimonies of many people who have been touched by the power of God. Many found it easy to receive from God, but others struggled and found it hard to freely receive. Below are some of the reasons why I believe some people hesitate to make themselves vulnerable before God, as well as the testimonies of people who themselves found it hard to receive from God, but reached a place of breakthrough.

❧❧ ❧❧

First of all, it is important to understand that we receive a touch from God in the same way that we receive anything from God: by faith. It has nothing to do with feelings.

Though we may well *feel* something when it happens, faith is the key element to receiving from God. The way to receive *more* from God than we are presently experiencing is simply to go to Him and *ask* for more. If we ask Him, He is willing to come and fill us. It sounds simple, doesn't it? And actually it is! So often we complicate things and make them more difficult than they need to be.

My wife, Carol, is what I affectionately refer to as a "lightning rod" of the Holy Spirit. She is so open and receptive to the power of God that whenever she is prayed for she will be mightily touched and will usually fall on the floor. I, on the other hand, tend to be towards the other end of the scale. In the past people have prayed for me until they were exhausted and still nothing happened. Often I would stand there, quietly observing other people basking in God's presence and think to myself, "I sure would like some of what they're getting," but still nothing happened.

I was certainly not alone in this. Over the years, having observed many thousands of people being prayed for, it has become evident that about a third of people receive a touch from God very easily, a third take a bit longer to be touched by God, and a third have quite a hard time receiving from Him at all. I was definitely in this last category.

I hasten to add that there isn't necessarily anything "wrong" with those people who find it hard. It's just a fact. Some people will fall down on the floor and spend hours in God's presence, later testifying to having been amazingly touched by God. Others listen to that and can't understand how it happens, and secretly wonder what might be wrong with them that they can't receive in that way.

The realization of this caused me to look at some of the things that I was doing, largely unconsciously, that were hindering me from freely receiving from the Holy Spirit. I discovered that in my heart there were several barriers in operation. The first was a fear-control barrier, of which there are several aspects listed below. There was also a pride-control barrier at work. And, lastly, there was simply the barrier of my own mind – how my thought processes worked and how that affected me.

Different people may be affected by one or all of these dynamics to different degrees, depending on their personality, but we need to deal with these issues in order to position ourselves to freely receive what God has for us. Fear, pride and wrong thinking war against us having true freedom in the Spirit, but God is calling us to intimacy and we need to respond to Him.

THE BARRIER OF FEAR

1. Fear of emotions

I mentioned earlier that culturally Western society has a fear of emotions/emotionalism hanging over it that is not shared by other nations. This fear of emotion has seeped into the Church and affected the people of God so that we have become suspicious of any kind of emotional response that occurs when God moves. And yet, who gave us our emotions? God did. He made us in His image and likeness and gave us the capacity to have and express emotions just as He does.

Galatians 5:22 says,

> *"The fruit of the Spirit is love, joy, peace, patience, kindness, goodness, faithfulness, gentleness and self-control. Against such things there is no law."*

People who are wary of emotionalism tend to quote this scripture a lot and state the fact that self-control is a fruit of the Spirit. That is true, but to be balanced one has to accept that other fruits listed here have a high emotional content to them. If, for example, the Holy Spirit fills your life with His love, what does that love look like? It's emotional! Imagine expressing a kind of love that has had all the emotion and feeling stripped out of it. What have you got left? Not much. What about joy? Is it possible to experience emotionless joy? – a "deep" joy, that's so deep you can't actually tell it's there?! At times we get so spiritually minded that we put no value on emotion, yet God created us with this capacity to experience emotion in order to add color and texture to our lives. At times Jesus cried and at other times He laughed. He prayed specifically for His disciples that they would have the same joy as He did and that their joy would be full. So we cannot disregard experiences of God that are infused with emotion.

Those who preach self-control will say that anything that seems to be out of control cannot be of God. I would temper that by saying, when the Holy Spirit moves upon a person and, for a time, they seem to be out of control, please don't take that "snapshot" of their life and use it to judge their *whole* life. Instead we need to see the bigger picture and understand how this touch of God has transformed them; how it has affected their relationship with Jesus, their marriage, their family, their church . . .

The point is not that someone fell on the floor and had an experience of the Holy Spirit. The point is: did this experience produce fruit in their life? Further investigation might reveal that, far from being out of control, this person now has evidence of the fruit of self-control in their life more than ever before. So just as we would not take a Polaroid of Jesus on the day He angrily cleansed the temple using a whip and accuse Him of being out of control and carnal, neither can we accuse individuals based on a single event.

In 1 Corinthians 12:7 Paul writes about the gifts of the Spirit being given to the Body of Christ in order to benefit it corporately:

"Now to each one the manifestation of the Spirit is given for the common good..."

The principle in Scripture is that wherever the Holy Spirit moves He will do good and produce spiritual fruit. When the Holy Spirit comes, if it is really Him, the resultant fruit will be very good: the Body of Christ will be lifted up, the Church will be encouraged, lives will be transformed, marriages will be healed. We can identify any true work of God by the fact that it will always point to and glorify Jesus.

The fear of emotion was a problem for me personally. I had never given myself permission to express my feelings very much. I can remember when I was about ten years old, crying over some issue, and my father saying to me, "Stop that! Men don't cry. Grow up!" At that point I put a big lid on my emotions and stuffed them way down inside. I said to myself, "OK, I won't express those feelings" and for years I didn't. But that is denial and we can't deny the very thing that God has made us to be. How can we truly relate to God if we are shut down emotionally?

I am not saying we should throw away our brains and let our emotions lead us. We would never do that in our marriages, for example. But then can you imagine a marriage without *any* emotions? I can't. We need to repent of our cultural misunderstandings about emotion and know that it's OK with God whether we laugh, cry or shout for joy in His presence.

2. Fear of deception

Many Christians seem to have a fear of being deceived by a demonic counterfeit of a real, God-given spiritual encounter and this single tool of the enemy has been used effectively as a weapon during moves of God past and present. If the enemy can put a fear of deception in our heart, causing us to pull back and withdraw, then he has robbed us of the faith we need to press in and receive a new infilling of the Holy Spirit. We need to believe that God has more power to bless us than the devil has to deceive us and have a childlike expectation that He will touch us afresh.

In Matthew 18:1–5 Jesus laid out this core principle of childlikeness as a key to receiving the kingdom:

> *"At that time the disciples came to Jesus and asked, 'Who is the greatest in the kingdom of heaven?'*
>
> *He called a little child and had him stand among them. And he said: 'I tell you the truth, unless you change and become like little children, you will never enter the kingdom of heaven. Therefore, whoever humbles himself like this child is the greatest in the kingdom of heaven. And whoever welcomes a little child like this in my name welcomes me.' "*

It is so important that we come to God in simplicity and not with great complexity! Have you ever thought about how complicated we make life for ourselves? Jesus tells us that what is needed is a basic, simple trust in God our Father. He elaborates on this principle in Luke 11:11–13:

> *"Which of you fathers, if your son asks for a fish, will give him a snake instead? Or if he asks for an egg, will give him a scorpion? If you then, though you are evil, know how to give good gifts to your children, how much more will your Father in heaven give the Holy Spirit to those who ask him!"*

Just as every good parent wants the best for their kids, so God wants the best for us. It is only the fear of deception that makes us think otherwise. We need to repent of this and break it out of our lives.

3. Fear of phenomena
John 18:6 recounts the story of Jesus' betrayal and capture in the garden at Gethsemane. Jesus asked the soldiers who

were coming to arrest Him, "Who are you looking for?" When they replied, "Jesus of Nazareth," Jesus said, *"I am He."* As He uttered those words, revealing His identity as God the Son, the men were flung backwards as the Holy Spirit hit them.

The truth is, whenever the Holy Spirit shows up powerful manifestations occur, but people are afraid of that. Christians have this preconceived notion that if something is really of God then we won't be afraid. We also have inherited this notion that the Holy Spirit is a Gentleman and will never force Himself upon us or make us do anything we don't want to do.

Consequently, when people see the phenomena of manifestations they withdraw and say, "That can't be of God." But our preconceptions don't match up with Scripture. Accounts in Scripture, like this one in John's Gospel and the story of Saul's conversion on the road to Damascus, prove that God can and will move upon a person without their permission. In addition, every time the Bible speaks of God manifesting His presence to human beings we read these words: fear not! Repeatedly an angel of the Lord will tell a terrified person, "Don't be afraid ... fear not..." which must mean that when God reveals His awesome presence to men they become very afraid.

4. Past hurts and fears

Another factor that can hinder people receiving from the Holy Spirit is fear arising out of past hurt. Over many years of counseling people I have heard some horror stories of the pain and abuse that people have suffered, especially when they were children. The result of these terrible events in their life is that they teach the heart of a child never to trust anyone, and as adults people are still controlled by this fear.

Naturally, someone who has experienced emotional trauma will find it hard to make themselves totally vulnerable before God. As they see people falling to the floor around them no doubt they are saying to themselves, "No way! I'm not going to be vulnerable like that!" because life has taught them that if they don't watch their back they will get hurt every time. But the wounds of past hurts like this will prevent us from receiving all that God has for us if they are not dealt with. We need to repent of responding to God out of the wrong kind of fear and ask Him to come and heal us.

Many thousands of people who visited us in Toronto received wonderful healings from deep wounds from their past right on the carpet of our church whilst under the power of the Holy Spirit. If there is one Person in the world we can trust, it must be Him! We can be vulnerable to the Holy Spirit because He will not hurt us. He only wants to heal us, build us up and encourage us.

5. Wrong theology

Lastly, some, through wrong teaching, have been led to believe that the gifts and operation of the Holy Spirit are not for today and were used by God only in the establishment His Church. Naturally, those coming from this point of view don't expect to see spiritual manifestations happening today. Yet, the evidence in Scripture for the present-day operation of the gifts is overwhelming.

Isn't it interesting that people believe Satan can demonstrate his power and, in some cases, even heal people, and at the same time they believe that the Holy Spirit can't or at least doesn't. Yet Jesus' mandate, not just to His immediate group of disciples but to all His disciples in all ages, was, "As the Father sent me, so I send you..."

Theologians who take this dispensational view of the Holy Spirit have constructed complex theological arguments to explain their point of view. Other books have dealt with these issues clearly and it's not my purpose to discuss the theological arguments here. But to me the Bible is clear: we are to do the same works as Jesus did. The same Holy Spirit who empowered His life empowers ours. Theology is something that was invented by man to try to contain and explain all that we know about God, but we must not allow our limited understanding to get in the way of actually knowing Him and experiencing Him in our lives.

THE BARRIER OF PRIDE

Just as fear leading to control will inhibit our openness towards God, so will pride. Pride also causes us to put in place control mechanisms in our life so that we never feel vulnerable or exposed. But such control only helps to shut down our intimacy with God. We need humility and repentance to break free from pride.

Society has placed a high value on looking cool. People want to be seen to be "on top" of their lives – to have it all worked out. No one wants to be seen as "needy" or lacking direction in their life. People with that kind of pride find falling on the floor and being totally open to God really difficult, because their pride is a barrier. Some think that as a Christian everything in their life should be fine, and that they should have no issues or problems; they don't want to appear to be in need because they find that embarrassing. Others just don't want to appear to be out of control because they find the very thought of exhibiting a loss of self-control embarrassing in itself. Either way the result is the same – both are limiting their intimacy with God and therefore limiting His ability to bless them.

THE BARRIER OF THE MIND

Apart from fear and pride, one of the greatest barriers to receiving from God is our mind. In 1 Corinthians 2 Paul teaches that the natural mind cannot perceive or understand the things of the Spirit of God. Paul, himself a highly educated man who had more reason than most to boast about his academic understanding, made a conscious decision to overcome the barrier of his mind when it came to the power of the Holy Spirit. In the opening verses of this chapter he says,

> *"When I came to you, brothers, I did not come with eloquence or superior wisdom as I proclaimed to you the testimony about God. For I resolved to know nothing while I was with you except Jesus Christ and him crucified. I came to you in weakness and fear, and with much trembling. My message and my preaching were not with wise and persuasive words, but with a demonstration of the Spirit's power, so that your faith might not rest on men's wisdom, but on God's power."*
>
> (1 CORINTHIANS 2:1–5)

Paul realized that there was little value in dazzling people with your knowledge and oratory skills, but that what really counted was God touching people's lives and transforming them by His power. In God's economy wisdom does not come before power, it works the other way around. Later, in verses 13–14 of this passage he writes,

> *"This is what we speak, not in words taught us by human wisdom but in words taught by the Spirit, expressing spiritual truths in spiritual words. The man without the Spirit does not accept the things that come from the Spirit of God, for they are foolishness to him, and he cannot understand them, because they are spiritually discerned."*

The fact is, we will never find God with our minds, only our hearts, because at the center of God's interaction with mankind is a divine romance. Our relationship with God is a matter of the heart. The intellectual pursuit of God ultimately leads to only one truth – that He is love!

God has always and will continue to do things that we will never fully comprehend or understand. But, if we go to Him in humility and ask Him to show us what is going on He will give us revelation. I am not dismissing the use of our minds altogether, because the mind of man has its place, but it should never be our primary method of seeking God.

My mind was a hindrance to me receiving from God because I habitually analyzed and rationalized all that was happening and that prevented me from coming into a place of intimacy with Him. Whenever someone would come and pray for me I would be saying, "Yes, Lord" with my mouth, but my eyes would be roaming around the room and my mind thinking, "I wonder what's happening over there." Carol, who is very spiritually sensitive, could detect when she was praying for me the difference between when I was focusing on God and when I had "zoned out".

If we accept that the earthly institution of marriage is a picture of Christ's relationship with His Bride, then think about this: what kind of marriage is only based on intellectual interaction and has no connection of passion, no meaningful interaction other than words? It would be a cold and sterile one to say the least. No one would expect a marriage like that to work. Likewise, our relationship with God must also include emotional love that we can feel and express, something more than just words. Revelation 2:1–5 says,

"To the angel of the church in Ephesus write:

These are the words of him who holds the seven stars in his right hand and walks among the seven golden lampstands: I know your deeds, your hard work and your perseverance. I know that you cannot tolerate wicked men, that you have tested those who claim to be apostles but are not, and have

found them false. You have persevered and have endured hardships for my name, and have not grown weary. Yet I hold this against you: You have forsaken your first love. Remember the height from which you have fallen! Repent and do the things you did at first. If you do not repent, I will come to you and remove your lampstand from its place."

At first glance the church in Ephesus sounds like a great church. They had persevered, endured hardship, uncovered false apostles . . . But, they had forsaken their first love. Jesus said to them, "You used to love me so much, but look how far you have fallen. Now you just work for me." Many believers have confused faithful work with romance and intimacy. Jesus doesn't want us to work for Him, He wants us to be in love with Him. There is a vast difference.

God's ways are not our ways

Often God doesn't behave in the way we expect Him to and that troubles our minds. The story of Naaman (2 Kings 5:1–4) is a classic example. This celebrated general was suffering from leprosy. He was so desperate to get well again that he traveled to a foreign country and was prepared to part with large sums of money and do whatever was necessary to be healed. Yet it was all based on a rumor: a slave girl had told him that there was a prophet in Israel who could heal him of his disease. Naaman went to seek this prophet, Elisha, and eventually tracked him down.

When Naaman called at Elisha's house the prophet was completely disinterested! In fact, he didn't even come out to greet Naaman, the great Syrian general. Elisha told his servant to go out to speak to him and instructed him to tell Naaman to dip himself seven times in the Jordan river. Naaman was angry and upset about this. In effect he said, "How dare he? I could have taken a bath in cleaner rivers back home if that would have helped!" He was about to leave in anger when one of his servants pleaded with him: "My father, listen. If the prophet had asked you to do a hard thing, wouldn't you have done it?"

It was true, Naaman would have undertaken any heroic task asked of him. No doubt this would have helped him feel he was making a contribution to his healing. But do a simple thing like this? He couldn't understand it. Nevertheless, he was persuaded by his servant, did as the prophet commanded and was completely healed. Notice that once Naaman relented he did not try to renegotiate the terms of the agreement. He could have said, "Surely three times is enough?" or "Won't the Lord heal me if I dip myself seven times in a river back home?" We all like to try and negotiate the terms of our dealings with God, but it just doesn't work like that! I have lost count of the number of people who visited us in Toronto and told me that they resisted coming for a long time because they said to themselves, "If God wants to touch me He can do it right here." Theologically this is true, but the fact is, if God tells us to do something or go somewhere then we need to obey Him.

THE IMPORTANCE OF SOAKING

It is here that I would like to recommend what we refer to as "soaking" in the presence of God as a wonderful exercise to incorporate into your spiritual life and prayer time. What do I mean by soaking? What I mean is to intentionally immerse yourself into the presence of God with the expectation and faith that you are going to receive something from your Heavenly Father. Something good, like the Father's promised blessing from Acts 1:4–5. God wants you and me to be thoroughly immersed and baptized in the Holy Spirit. Years ago, many old saints referred to "tarrying" or waiting on God for answered prayer, or to be baptized in the Holy Spirit. This is precisely what I mean. Humble yourself and position yourself before God in a relaxed and restful position, such as sitting or even lying down on the floor. Put some worship music on and begin to enter into worshiping the Lord with all your heart and soul. We are invited to worship the Father in Spirit and in truth according to John 4:23–24. The Father is seeking those who will so worship Him in Spirit and in truth, and we want to be people who will do just that.

This is actually what works best for me. I need to go "off duty", so to speak, and begin to rest in the love of God. I will meditate on what Jesus did on the cross and the intense whipping that He took that I may be healed. I think about His death for me and His resurrection, also for me. I put music on, sometimes with words to help me focus and sometimes just instrumental so my heart can follow the leading of the Holy Spirit. I remind myself about the love of God and begin to have an intimate time together with Him. After about fifteen or twenty minutes of this I am at rest with His wonderful deep peace upon me. When I go to get up, I usually become aware of His heavy presence upon me. It is moments like these that draw us closer and enable us to receive the Father's love and blessing.

Steve Long, who is now our Senior Pastor in Toronto, tells how soaking led to a personal breakthrough for him. Feeling a little like the blessing of the Lord was passing him by while others were receiving profound spiritual experiences, Steve began to "soak" every morning for about twenty to thirty minutes. He would put his current favorite worship music on and lie down comfortably on the floor in his bedroom or living room. He didn't notice anything happening to him in particular, except that over the weeks he enjoyed and now looked forward to the peace and rest that was his portion from spending time with the Lord. But unknowingly, he was becoming more and more sensitive to the Holy Spirit's presence. One day when visiting speakers were ministering to our leaders, Steve simply said out loud, "Oh oh!" and fell over onto the floor. This was the first of many deep and wonderful encounters for Steve. He continues to enjoy soaking to this day as it is still a restful and peaceful way for him to enter into a divine encounter.

TESTIMONIES

In the remainder of this section I want to share a few stories of people who were wonderfully touched by God in our meetings, but who would describe themselves as previously finding it difficult to receive.

Bob had attended meetings on a number of occasions and had been prayed for many times. In fact, he counted up the number of times he was prayed for when nothing happened! He wanted to feel God's presence in a special, tangible way, but every time he felt nothing. Bob says,

> "I counted how many times I was prayed for – it was twenty-five times – and I didn't feel a thing. I was beginning to question whether I was really a Christian. I thought I was! Then God gave me a scripture in Colossians that says if you have been raised up in Christ keep seeking the things that are above, rather than what is on earth, so I said, OK, I'm coming to Toronto to get raised up in Christ – that was God's word to me.
>
> I got prayed for and nothing happened again. I didn't feel anything. I got so frustrated by this that I cried out to God, 'Lord, please will you lift me up!' and then, as clear as a bell, I heard Him speak back to me, 'I am lifting you up!' and it hit me. I asked Him, 'Lord, do you mean I don't have to feel anything?' I realized that receiving a touch from God is just like becoming a Christian – you just have to take it by faith, you don't have to feel anything.

I was happy then and I prayed, 'God, I receive whatever you've got for me by faith.' Then, last night when a guy came over to pray for me I started reassuring him saying, 'I'm probably not going to fall down, but that's OK.' He prayed for me for quite a while and I didn't expect anything to happen. But then, after a bit, my body started to sway. I thought to myself, 'Well, I've been standing up for 45 minutes, I'm just tired, that's all.' But my body kept on swaying and I realized, actually, it's not me doing this, I think I'll just give in to it. So I just let go and the next thing I knew, bang, I was down on the floor.

I lay on the floor and felt very peaceful. Then a guy also lying on the floor a couple of feet away from me began to laugh. After a while I started laughing at his laugh. I chuckled for a bit, but then I realized: this isn't regular laughter I'm experiencing here, this is beginning to increase in intensity. I laughed so hard I thought I was going to burst! And I remember thinking, this is glorious, it's wonderful. Praise God!"

One of the reasons we always ask to hear people's testimonies is so that other people can see how the Holy Spirit is working in the lives of others and so they can see that there is no manipulation taking place to encourage manifestations. We just ask God to come upon people powerfully and soak them in His presence. Often the most profound and appropriate prayer we can pray for a person is simply, "More, Lord" because God knows exactly what that person needs.

Connie had prayer for many consecutive weeks, wanting a fresh encounter with God and seemingly nothing happened. But she continued to press in to God. She says,

"When all this renewal stuff broke out in the church I watched everything happen: the people would laugh and fall down. I watched it, thinking that it was good, but I just didn't think that God would do that for me. So when people prayed for me I would just cry and that was about all that ever happened. After about three months of prayer though, one day I shook and felt totally drunk in the Spirit and even the next morning when I got up, all I had to say was "Jesus" and I was out again...

But then that didn't happen again and I became afraid, thinking that maybe it had just been me shaking. And I really shut down what God had done in me ... Another five or six months passed by and I had reached the place in my thinking where I believed that because other people laughed and fell over God must love them, but not me. So I had to come from there to a place in myself where I really believed that God was for me no matter what; whether anything happened to me when I was prayed for or not. I believed He could pour His life into me whether I was standing, sitting or whatever, and it wasn't dependent on me doing anything like shaking or falling over.

When I'd finally made this conscious decision in my mind to just press in after Jesus no matter what, I found that I could really allow Him to go deeper into my heart. I really began to receive from God then – and I also began to shake! But that didn't matter any more because it wasn't my focus. My focus wasn't on the manifestation, it was on Jesus and whatever He wanted to do."

Steve was a guy we knew who was always the life and soul of the party, but when it came to getting serious about God he was always on the sidelines and never felt a part of what was going on. He had a certain amount of pride that told him people only needed a touch from God because they were weak.

"I was always skeptical about the power of God. I had never felt the Lord before, until about a year ago. My wife was a worship leader at our church, but I never really attended. Often I would drop her and our kids off at church and then go to the coffee shop. Just occasionally I would turn up at church for the end of the service and talk to a few people. I couldn't understand why they were raising their hands all the time and so I would mock them a bit.

My wife would often go forward and she would get slain in the Spirit. I thought, well, she's weaker than I am and maybe she needs that. All I knew was I wanted to stay in control of my life.

Eventually I did go up for prayer at one of the meetings because I had been in a truck accident at work and I was suffering pain from the top of my back all the way down my legs. I used to have a hard time breathing. I went forward for prayer and one of the ministry team prayed for me. The next thing I knew I felt my feet go up above my head and I was on the floor! I didn't get up for the next three hours.

When I was down on the floor it felt as though my arms were being pulled and stretched out to either side. I can't explain it. Then I realized that for the first time in a long time I could breathe without experiencing any pain. The Lord didn't totally heal me at that time, but I was no longer in pain when I took a breath.

During this time God released me from a lot of fears I had in my life. I was worried that my father wasn't going to come to the Lord and go to Heaven. But God showed me how compassionate He is and He showed me a picture of Him cuddling my Dad in His arms like a baby and I was just crying and crying. I was so touched. I'm a guy who hasn't been used to crying, but the tears just came.

The second time I went for prayer the same thing happened. I was a bit worried that nothing would happen, but God just drew me. I got prayed for and fell down again and God did a number of things in me. I saw that God had so much love and mercy for me, and I just felt like I was being washed, that God was forgiving me for all my sins. God showed me one thing after another and I would cry and repent of it, then I knew that God was forgiving me for those things."

David, a vicar from the West coast of England, said the following:

"After reading a prophecy from Marc Dupont I booked a flight for myself and my associate minister and came to Toronto. I can't begin to tell you all that God did. I'd had a year off work with a head injury and my ministry had gone quite dry. Although I had been working again for about nine months at this point, things just weren't really ticking.

So I came to Toronto with quite an agenda, which God graciously ignored. I went home feeling as though I had been born again, again! During the time I was here, one of the things that the Lord said to me was that He wanted me to sort out my relationship with my wife, Lynn. I had taken a lot out of our relationship because of my invalidity during that year, but it had become a habit for me after I recovered. I went home and said sorry to her, repented and made an effort to sort things out.

One thing that happened as a result was that we began praying together a lot more. In fact, we have prayed more for our children in this last month than we have in twenty-one years of marriage. Praying with

Lynn was always something that I'd found hard to do. I
don't know why. I always hoped and expected that it
would be a natural, easy thing to do, but it wasn't. Now
I have such a renewed love for her and it's easy. Yes,
my love for Jesus has increased, but my love for my
wife has just gone through the roof!"

Each of these people experienced a powerful touch from
God during a fresh encounter with the Holy Spirit. But the
important thing to notice is that each of them is bearing
the fruit of the experience and that fruit is glorifying the
work of Jesus is their lives. This is the ultimate test of
whether God is working in a person's life.

In conclusion, it is not the manifestations of the Holy Spirit
working that are important normally, but the work that is
done by the Holy Spirit in a person's heart. Push past the
manifestations issue, see and desire the deep work that God
will do in your heart and the hearts of others, and press on
with faith and persistence for the blessing that is promised
to you (Acts 1:4).

APPENDIX

EMPIRICAL EVIDENCE FROM AN INDEPENDENT SURVEY

In late 1994 I was approached by a lady who had been attending our meetings who asked permission to conduct a survey amongst people who had been touched by God's power. Her name was Margaret Poloma (of the University of Akron and Vanguard University of Southern California, USA). Margaret is a sociologist by profession. I agreed to the survey and below is a short extract from the report she wrote after analyzing the results.

Margaret prefaced her report by saying, "I write not as a theologian but as a sociologist who attempts to use her research and perspective to contribute a kind of 'empirical theology' or 'theosociology' on our topic of interest. As a sociologist, I have played the role of a participant observer of the larger Pentecostal/Charismatic movement for over two decades ... "

Social Psychological Data

When I approached Toronto's pastor, John Arnott, with a plan to conduct a survey on pilgrims to the site, Arnott's immediate response was, "What can I do to help you?" He seemed as eager as I to secure some hard data ...

In 1995 we conducted a non-random survey distributed through the August issue of *Spread the Fire* magazine, through the October "Catch the Fire Again" program, and through the November "Healing School Program". Questionnaires were returned to the author at the University of Akron (Ohio) in the USA, with a place for the respondent to indicate whether he or she were willing to participate in a possible follow-up study. A total of 918 useable responses was received from 20 countries, with the largest number coming from the USA (54%), Canada (26%), and England (11%). Seventy-five percent provided a useable address for a follow-up survey conducted in May, 1997, that yielded data on 364 of the original respondents. While such non-random procedures do not permit generalizations to the hundreds of thousands of persons who visited Toronto during the ongoing renewal meetings, they do permit us to describe some of the possible effects Toronto has had on those respondents – conclusions that could, with caution, be extended to thousands of others who did not fill out the surveys. Responses to two sets of questions will be presented in this article: increases in personal empowerment and increases in service and outreach.

Personal Empowerment

The preliminary and exploratory questions asked in the 1995 survey indicated that the vast majority of the respondents (92%) had experienced the power of God and that it lasted even after leaving TACF. Presumably it was this fresh touch of the power of God that led 90 percent of them to invite others to come to TACF and 82 percent to report that evangelism was more important to them now than it had ever been before. The follow-up survey secured additional information on experiences of empowerment.

More than half of the 1997 respondents indicated an increase in receiving prophetic words (62%), while almost half reported an increase in receiving words of knowledge (47%), prophetic intercession (48%), and prophetic dreams (41%). Similar figures were reported for an increase in empowerment in praying for the physical and emotional healing of others since visiting the renewal in Toronto: 49 percent replied that their was an increase in emotional healing and 34 percent saw an increase in their efficacy in praying for physical healing. In sum, it would appear that many pilgrims to Toronto did experience a fresh release of charismatic gifts, particularly in the realm of the prophetic and healing, both of which are subjects of regular conferences conducted at TACF. Based on this survey it would be safe to say that many individuals who have visited TACF believed they were moving in a much greater power of the Spirit in 1997 than they were in pre-renewal days.

Increase in Service and Outreach

Another area of questioning in the 1997 survey that is relevant ... is whether renewal participants are moved to action as a result of the Blessing. We have already seen that many purport to be more effective in charismatic ministry, especially prophecy and healing. Other questions tapped an increase in service and outreach to the larger community.

Nine questions were asked to determine whether participants became more involved in outreach as a result of the renewal, with a mean or average of 3.6 and a median of 4. This statistic suggests that the model respondent increased his or her service for approximately 4 of the listed items. Those experiencing the Toronto Blessing reported themselves to be more likely to offer assistance to friends (64%) or acquaintances (57%) as a result of their Toronto experience. They were more likely to increase their service to the church (55%), giving financially to missions (44%) and to the poor (35%), visiting the sick (34%), efforts to lead others to Christ (25%), to reach out to the poor and homeless (24%), and to be involved in other works of mercy (20%).

There appears to be a relatively strong relationship between experiencing an increase in empowerment and reporting an increase in outreach to others ($r = .32$). Those who have been more effective in prayers of prophecy and healing are more likely to report an increase in outreach and service. While these are personal data and self reports, they do suggest that there are countless individuals whose ministries have been enhanced as a result of their experience of the Toronto Blessing. It appears that the Blessing has empowered and activated many for service.

About the Author

John and Carol Arnott are the Founding Pastors at Toronto Airport Christian Fellowship (TACF). They live in Toronto and travel extensively while continuing to pastor TACF.

An international speaker and teacher, John Arnott is known for his ministry of the Lord's forgiveness and mercy. John attended Ontario Bible College. He then pursued a varied and successful career in business. In 1980, while on a ministry trip to Indonesia, John responded to God's call on his life for full-time ministry. John and Carol were the founding pastors of Jubilee Christian Fellowship in Stratford, Ontario. They started the Toronto church in 1988.

Experience as a businessman, husband, father and pastor, has given John a rich, blended ministry of God's grace, healing and deliverance. He puts special emphasis on the Father heart of God, which has impacted many people with God's life-changing love and grace. John has authored several books including *The Father's Blessing, Experience the Blessing, The Importance of Forgiveness* and *Revolutionizing Faith*. John is a director of the TACF church network, Partners in Harvest, and the general editor of TACF's bi-monthly magazine *Spread the Fire*.

John and Carol invest much of their time imparting God's love and power to people in many different cities and nations through conferences and special revival meetings.

CONTACT
INFORMATION

Spread the Fire Ministries
272 Attwell Drive
Toronto
Ontario
M9W 6M3
Canada

www.johnandcarol.org

For more information regarding TACF in Toronto, go to
www.tacf.org
or
www.ctfMinistries.com

We hope you enjoyed reading this New Wine book.
For details of other New Wine books
and a wide range of titles from other
Word and Spirit publishers visit our website:
www.newwineministries.co.uk
email: newwine@xalt.co.uk